Contents

All about bags and purses 4

Didgeridoo pencil case 6

Mini parfleche 8

Funky wallet 10

MP3-player bag 12

Hallowe'en bag 14

Drawstring gym bag 16

Magic wallet 18

Magazine bag 20

Glossary 22

Further information 23

Index 24

All about bags & purses

We use bags and purses every day for carrying and storing things and keeping things safe. Bags and purses come in many shapes and sizes, from small wallets to bigger gym kit bags.

BAGS FROM LONG AGO

People have used bags and purses throughout history. The Ancient Romans used a drawstring leather pouch that was hung from a belt to hold their heavy coins. The Ancient Egyptians made baskets and bags from materials such as reeds and grasses. The Native Americans made a pouch, known as a parfleche, from buffalo hide (see right) to keep their belongings safe.

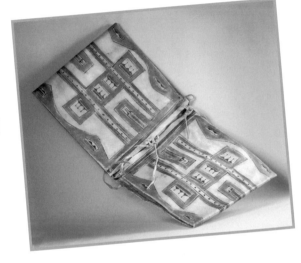

For a time, pouches were worn on the outside of clothes, tied on around the waist, like a Scottish sporran (see left). A sporran is a pouch attached to a belt and worn over a kilt. Pouches on the outside were often snatched so people began to wear them under their clothes. Today, it is not just money that people keep safe in bags – mobile telephones, walkmans and MP3 players are all carried in bags of different shapes and sizes.

DIFFERENT MATERIALS

Modern bags and purses are made from a variety of materials, depending on their use. Some bags, such as rucksacks (see right) and briefcases, are waterproof. This means that the things inside them will stay dry on a rainy day. Handbags and wallets are often made from leather so that they last a long time. The leather can also be dyed so the bags and wallets come in lots of different colours. Other bags, such as grocery carrier bags, are made from a type of plastic. Plastic bags are not only strong so that you can put lots of things in them, but often they can be recycled, so they are good for the environment, too.

GET STARTED!

This book shows you how to make different bags and purses. When you make your projects, try to use materials that you already have either at home or at school. For example, for card, use the back of finished notepads, artpads and empty cereal boxes. For the fabric in these projects, old, but clean clothes, pillowcases, bedsheets and towels are ideal. Reusing and recycling materials like this is good for the environment and will save you money. The projects have all been made and decorated for this book but do not worry if yours look a little different — just have fun making and using your bags and purses.

Didgeridoo pencil case

The didgeridoo is a musical instrument used by the Aboriginal people of Australia. Didgeridoos are made from the branches of eucalyptus trees that have been hollowed out by termites. Follow the steps to make your own didgeridoo-style pencil case.

YOU WILL NEED

coloured paper
empty biscuit or sweet tube with lid
pair of scissors
pencil
spare paper
newspaper
paints
paintbrush
double-sided tape

1 Cut a sheet of coloured paper large enough to wrap around the tube.

2 Think about the patterns and pictures you want as part of your design. Do some rough drawings onto spare paper.

3 When you are happy with your design, draw it onto the coloured paper cut in Step 1.

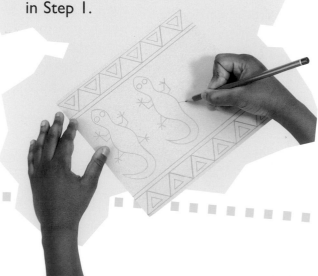

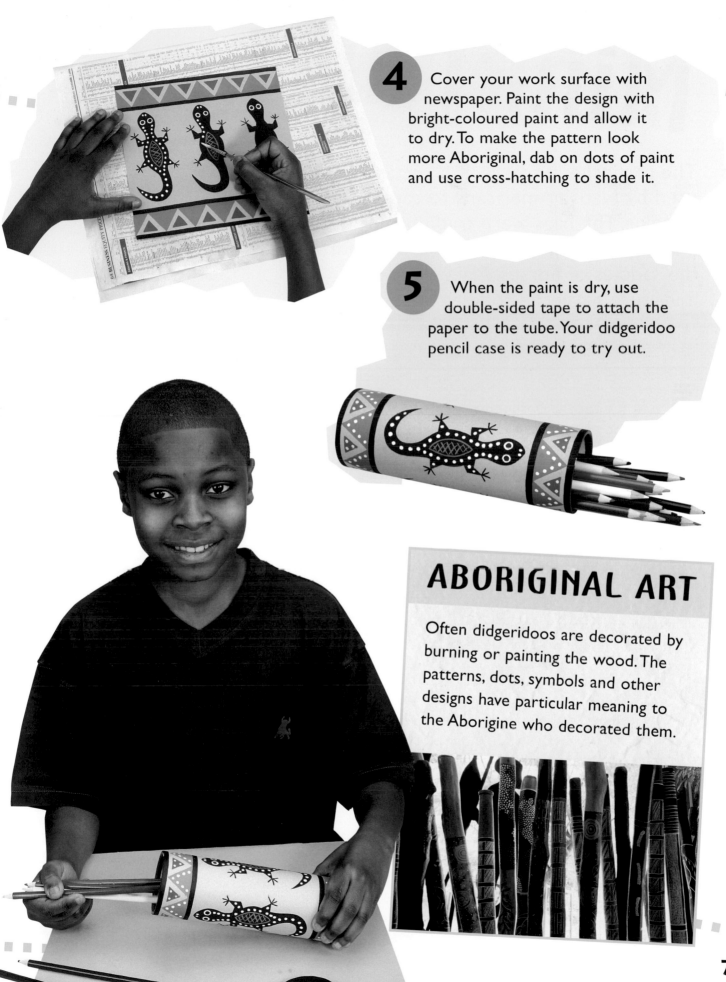

4 Cover your work surface with newspaper. Paint the design with bright-coloured paint and allow it to dry. To make the pattern look more Aboriginal, dab on dots of paint and use cross-hatching to shade it.

5 When the paint is dry, use double-sided tape to attach the paper to the tube. Your didgeridoo pencil case is ready to try out.

ABORIGINAL ART

Often didgeridoos are decorated by burning or painting the wood. The patterns, dots, symbols and other designs have particular meaning to the Aborigine who decorated them.

Mini parfleche

The parfleche is a large, flat, rectangular bag used by Native Americans to carry food and clothing. The bags were traditionally made from buffalo hide and they were hung from the saddles of horses. Make your own miniature parfleche to keep your things safe.

YOU WILL NEED

light-coloured A3 card

black felt-tip pen

ruler

pair of scissors

hole punch

pencil

coloured pencils

string or shoelace

1 Place the card with shortest sides at the top and bottom. Using a black felt-tip pen and ruler, draw a line across the card that is that is 11cm from the top of the card and a line that is 11cm from the bottom of the card. Then draw a line 8cm in from the right-hand side and another line 8cm in from the left-hand side of the card.

2 Draw lines across the corners of the card where the lines meet the edge of the card. Cut across these lines so that you have an octagon (eight-sided shape).

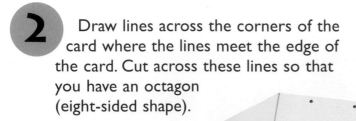

3 Use a hole punch to make holes where shown.

4 Turn the card over so that the lines are face down. Use a pencil to draw a geometric pattern onto the longer inner section of the card. Go over the design with a black felt-tip pen and colour it in with coloured pencils.

5 Turn the card over so that the pattern is facing down. Fold the longer sides in along the lines drawn in Step 1. Put the things you are keeping in the parfleche underneath the flaps. Thread some string through the holes and tie the sides together.

6 Fold over the short ends along the lines drawn in Step 1. Tie these ends together to keep your things safe.

NATIVE AMERICANS

The Native Americans lived on the Great Plains area of North America, alongside rivers and streams. They hunted the animals, such as buffalo, that roamed the plains. The animals were killed for food and they also provided the Native Americans with hides to make clothing.

Funky wallet

A wallet is a pocket-sized bag. Usually, wallets have different sections for holding paper money, cards and coins. Reuse an old plastic tablecloth to make your own new wallet.

YOU WILL NEED

pencil
ruler
old plastic tablecloth
pair of scissors
strong tape
string glue
velcro, 6cm long

1 Use a pencil and ruler to draw the following shapes onto the tablecloth: two rectangles at 25cm x 12cm, one rectangle at 7cm x 28cm and two squares at 8cm x 8cm. Cut out all the shapes.

2 Using the picture as a guide, stick tape along edges, covering the patterned side by about 1.5cm.

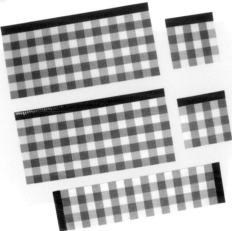

3 To make a coin pouch, place the 7cm x 28cm rectangle pattern-side down with the short edge at the top and bottom. Fold up the rectangle from the bottom by 11cm.

4 Place one of the 25cm x 12cm rectangles pattern-side up and with the taped edge away from you. Put the coin pouch in the middle of the rectangle and tape it down the sides.

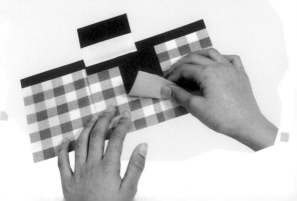

5 Place one of the square pieces of tablecloth pattern-side up on the left-hand side of the coin pouch. Align the pieces at the bottom. Tape down the square along the right-hand side, overlapping the square piece by about 1.5cm. Repeat this with the other square on the right-hand side, taping it down on the left-hand side.

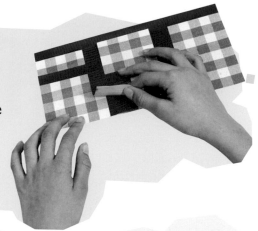

6 Lay the second 25cm x 12cm rectangle pattern-side down and with the taped edge away from you. Place the rectangle from step 5 pattern-side up on top and tape the two together along the sides and bottom edge, overlapping the pocketed side by about 1.5cm.

7 Use strong glue to stick one half of the velcro to the underside of the coin pouch flap. Glue the other half of the velcro to the middle of the coin pouch, so that when the flap is closed the two halves meet. Your wallet is now ready to use.

FANTASTIC PLASTIC

Plastic is a tough, waterproof material. It is used to make all kinds of things, from toys and toothbrushes to telephones and bottles. Plastic was accidentally discovered by J Paul Hogan and Robert L Banks while they were trying to make fuel. During their experiments, they realised that their machines had become blocked with a sticky white substance. This white substance became known as plastic.

11

MP3-player bag

This pocket-sized bag is similar to the Celtic bags worn by men, called sporrans. But this bag is not going on a belt. Instead it is small enough to fit snugly in your pocket.

YOU WILL NEED

felt
pair of scissors
button
pencil or chalk
needle
embroidery thread
fun fur
tassels

1 Cut a length of felt that will wrap around your MP3 player one and a half times and is 4cm wider than the player.

2 Use the pair of scissors to round off one end of the felt. This will become the flap end of the bag.

3 Place the felt with the rounded end away from you and place your MP3 player in the middle. Fold the felt up from the bottom so that it covers the MP3 player.

4 Mark where you would like the button to be with a pencil or chalk. Sew the button in place (see page 13).

5 Lay the fabric down in front of you with the button side down and rounded end away from you. Fold it up from the bottom by enough to cover the MP3 player. Make a mark so you know how far up this is.

6 Using a running stitch (see page 16) sew the two layers together along one side, up to the mark you made in in Step 5. Sew 1cm in from the edge. Turn back and repeat the running stitch through the stitches already sewn.

SEWING ON BUTTONS

1. Thread a needle and knot one end.
2. Hold the button where you want it to be. Push the needle up from underneath the fabric and up through one hole of the button.
3. Take the needle down through the diagonally opposite hole and through the fabric.
4. Repeat this 3–4 times through the same holes.
5. Do the same through the other two holes.
6. Take the thread back through to underneath the fabric and knot it.

7 Sew up the other side in the same way.

8 Fold down the flap and feel where it covers the centre of the button. Mark this with a pencil or chalk. Make a snip with the scissors that is long enough for the button to go through.

9 Sew on a small piece of fun fur and add some tassels to decorate your bag. It is now ready to try out. You could make a bag in the same way for a mobile telephone.

Hallowe'en bag

What we know as Hallowe'en was originally part of the Celtic celebration of New Year, known as Samhain. Today on Hallowe'en, people carve pumpkins and many children dress up in costumes, going from door to door trick or treating. Follow these simple steps to make your own pumpkin-shaped treat bag to hold all your goodies.

YOU WILL NEED

A3 size orange artfoam
pencil
ruler
pair of scissors
small plate
stapler
black artfoam
double-sided tape

1 From the long edge of the orange artfoam, measure and cut out a strip that is 10cm wide and 40cm long. From the remaining artfoam, cut two circles that are about 20cm in diameter. You may find it helpful to draw around a plate for this.

2 Place the edge of one circle against the edge of the strip of artfoam. Staple them together, about 1cm in from the edge. Continue stapling around the circle, keeping the edges together.

3 Staple on the second circle in the same way.

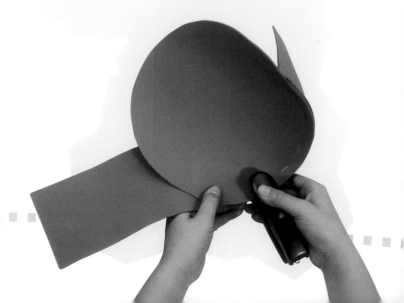

4 Draw and cut out shapes at the opened end of both circles to make handles.

THE LIGHT SEASON

The Celtic year was divided into two seasons: the light and the dark. The last day of October was the end of the light season and the end of the year. The Celts believed that on 31 October, the dead would visit the places where they used to live. To protect themselves and to scare away unfriendly spirits, the Celts carved images into turnips. Today on Hallowe'en, people carve pumpkins instead.

5 To give your pumpkin bag a face, cut out eye, nose and mouth shapes from the black artfoam. Using double-sided tape, stick them to the bag. Your bag is ready to fill with delicious treats!

You could change the colour and decorations on this bag to make a bag for Easter or Christmas.

Drawstring gym bag

Small drawstring bags were originally used for carrying coins. Gradually, the bags became bigger and in the 18th and 19th centuries, ladies would carry their handkerchiefs in drawstring bags called reticules. Follow the steps to makes your own drawstring gym bag.

YOU WILL NEED

fabric 35cm x 90cm

thread

sewing needle

pair of scissors

180cm piping cord

safety pin

1 Fold the fabric in half with the right sides facing each other.

GET SEWING

To sew a running stitch, start by threading a needle. Tie a knot at one end of the thread. Push the point of the needle down through the fabric. Bring the needle back up again at a point further forward from where you went down. Repeat this to give a row of stitches which look the same on both sides of the fabric.

2 Knot one end of the thread and thread the other end onto the needle. Sew a running stitch along one side of the fabric 2cm in from the edge, starting at the folded edge. Stop stitching about 7cm from the top. Turn back and repeat the running stitch through the stitches already sewn. When you reach the end, knot the thread to keep it in place. Sew up the other side of the bag in the same way.

3 Turn the bag inside out so that the fabric is the correct way around. Taking one side at a time, turn the top over to the inside by 3cm and sew a running stitch all along, 2cm from the top. Turn back and repeat the running stitch through the stitches already sewn. This will make a tube for the cord to pass through.

4 Snip a hole 4–5cm in from the bottom corner of one side of the bag. Thread one end of the piping cord through the hole and knot it tightly around the corner.

5 Attach a safety pin to the other end of the cord. Place it in the tube at the top of the bag on the same side as the knot. Wriggle the safety pin and cord along the tube around both sides of the bag.

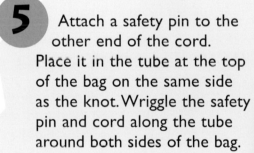

6 Bring the cord back out at the side where you started and take it back to the corner. Unhook the safety pin and thread the cord through the hole. Knot it tightly around the corner. Your bag is ready to try – put some trainers in the bag and sling it over your shoulder!

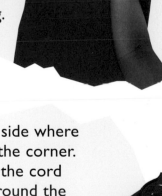

Magic wallet

Keep your money and cards in this wallet. Be warned though, this wallet has magical properties and you may find that your money is not where you left it!

YOU WILL NEED

2 pieces of card, 8cm x 11cm

sticky-backed plastic, fabric or wrapping paper

glue (if using fabric or wrapping paper)

pair of scissors

ruler

length of 5mm wide elastic, 80cm long

stapler

1 Cover each side of both pieces of card with sticky-backed plastic, fabric or paper. When dry, lay the two rectangles next to each other.

2 Staple one end of the elastic to the top left-hand edge of the left card, 3cm down from the top.

3 Take the elastic under the left-hand card and over the top of the right-hand card. Staple it in place, slightly stretching the elastic.

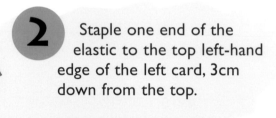

4 Take the elastic diagonally across the back of the right-hand card and across the front of the left-hand card.

5 Staple the elastic in place as shown.

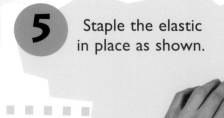

6 Take the elastic under the bottom of the left-hand card and over the top at the bottom of the right-hand card. Staple it in place.

7 Take the elastic behind and diagonally across back of the card and bring it back out at the top of card but below the earlier elastic. Staple it in place but make sure you do not staple the elastic running behind the card. Cut off any spare elastic.

8 Turn over the wallet and you should have one side with an 'x' of elastic. On the other side, you should have two parallel lines.

9 Try out the wallet by placing something under the 'x' or the parallel lines, then flip the other side over and over again. The card magically moves under the parallel elastic!

Magazine bag

Use an old pillowcase to make a bag for carrying some of your favourite magazines and comic books. You will need an adult to help you with some of the steps in this project.

YOU WILL NEED

clean, old pillowcase

pair of scissors

pencil or piece of chalk

ruler

20mm wide iron-on hemming tape

iron and ironing board

1 Turn your pillowcase inside out. Use scissors to cut off the stitching from either side of the pillowcase, keeping as close to the edge of the stitching as possible. Open out the pillowcase.

2 Cut a 60cm width of fabric from one end of the opened pillowcase. This will make the main part of the bag. From the remaining fabric, cut two strips that are 10cm wide and as long as the fabric. These will make the two handles.

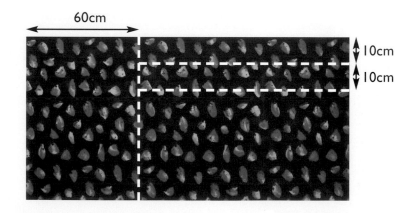

60cm

10cm

10cm

3 Cut two lengths of iron-on hemming tape the same length as the handles. Place the handles in front of you with the wrong sides up. Put the hemming tape along the edge of each handle. Fold each handle in half along the length. Ask an adult to iron the fabric and hemming tape, following the instructions on the packet.

4 Cut two lengths of hemming tape the same length as the shortest side of the main part of the bag. Place the rectangle of fabric in front of you with the wrong side up and the shortest side at the top. Turn over the top edge by 3cm. Place a strip of hemming tape underneath the fold.

Try to be creative with old linen by reusing and recycling it to make bags and purses. Can you think of ways to decorate your bag with the left-over fabric? Perhaps you could cut out and sew on a pocket? Or you could make a matching draw-string pouch for your mobile telephone.

5 Place the ends of one of the straps on top of the hemming tape, making sure the strap is not twisted. Lay the second piece of hemming tape on top. Turn down the fold of fabric. Ask an adult to iron the fold in place.

6 Ask an adult to help you iron the second strap to the other end of the rectangle in the same way.

7 Bend the straps up and ask an adult to iron a double layer of hemming tape between the straps and the top of the bag to hold the straps in place.

8 Fold the bag up with the right sides together. Place a double layer of hemming tape between the fabric along one side of the bag. Ask an adult to iron on the hemming tape. Repeat for the other side, and then turn the bag inside out.

21

Glossary

Aborigine
A person who lived in Australia before the Europeans settled there. There are still Aboriginal people living in Australia today.

Celtic
Belonging to the people who lived in Britain before the Romans settled there.

didgeridoo
A musical instrument that is traditionally played by the Aborigines of Australia.

eucalyptus tree
A very tall evergreen tree found in Australia. The oil from the eucalyptus leaf is often used in medicines.

experiment
A scientific test that is done to see what happens.

fuel
Something that is burnt to make heat or power, such as coal or oil.

Hallowe'en
The festival that happens each year on 31 October. Hallowe'en was traditionally part of the Celtic New Year celebrations.

hide
The skin of an animal.

kilt
A kind of pleated skirt that is traditionally worn by Scottish men.

kit
The special clothes and shoes that a person uses to play sport. For example, a football kit consists of a shirt, shorts, boots and shin pads.

material
Anything used for making something else. Leather, metal, wood and plastic are all materials.

Native Americans
The people who live on the Great Plains area of North America. Native Americans are divided into several different tribes, including the Cheyenne and the Sioux.

recycling
To recycle something is to change it or treat it so that it can be used again. For example, the metal in drinks cans can be recycled into other metal things.

reusing

To use something for a different purpose. For example, if you use the cardboard from a cereal packet to make a project, you are reusing the cardboard.

running stitch

A simple stitch where the thread is worked in and out of the fabric. The stitches can be short or long.

sporran

A pouch that is worn by Scottish men at the front of their kilt. Sporrans are usually made of leather and covered in fur.

termite

An insect that is known for eating through wood. Sometimes, termites are called white ants.

trick or treating

The game children play at Hallowe'en when they knock on people's doors asking for treats. If people do not give the children sweets or other treats, the children play a trick on them.

waterproof

Something that water cannot get into. Some materials, such as certain types of plastic, are waterproof.

FURTHER INFORMATION

www.didgeridoos.net.au/aboriginal-symbols.html
   This website has lots of different Aboriginal art symbols for you to use to decorate your pencil case.

www.morningstargallery.com/parfleche/index.html
   The Morning Star Gallery has an online exhibition of Native American art and artefacts. There are many different parfleches to inspire you when you make yours.

http://hcms.firstoption.net/peach2cms/SiteResources/hcms_bags.jsp
   Use this link to look at handbags throughout history, from leather and fabric bags to snakeskin and beaded bags.

Note to parents and teachers:

The website addresses (URLs) included in this book were valid at the time of going to press. However, because of the nature of the Internet, it is possible that some addresses may have changed, or sites may have changed or closed down since publication. While the author and publishers regret any inconvenience this may cause the readers, no responsibility for any such changes can be accepted by either the author or the publisher.

Index

A
Aboriginal art 7
Aborigines 6, 7, 22
Ancient Egypt 4, 21, 22
Ancient Rome 4
Australia 6

B
Banks, Robert L 11
baskets 4
belts 4
briefcases 4
buffalo 4, 8, 9

C
carrier bags 5
Celtic 12, 14, 15, 22
clothes 4, 8, 9
comic books 20

D
didgeridoo pencil case 6–7
didgeridoos 6, 7, 22
drawstring bags 4, 16–17

E
environment 5, 21
eucalyptus trees 6, 22

F
food 8, 9
fuel 11, 22

H
Hallowe'en 14, 15, 22
Hallowe'en bag 14–15
handbags 5

hides 4, 8, 9, 22
Hogan, J Paul 11
horses 8

K
kilts 4, 22
kit bags 4

L
leather 4, 5

M
magazine bag 20–21
magic wallet 18–19
materials 4, 5, 22
mobile telephones 4, 13
money 4, 5, 10, 16, 18, 21
MP3-player bag 12–13
MP3 players 4
musical instruments 6

N
Native Americans 4, 8, 9, 22
North America 9

P
parfleche 4, 8–9
plastic 5, 10, 11
pouches 4, 21
pumpkins 14, 15

R
recycling 5, 21, 22
reticules 16
reusing 5, 10, 23
rucksacks 5

S
Samhain 14
Scotland 4
sewing 12, 13, 16, 23
sporran 4, 12, 23
symbols 7

T
termites 6, 23
trees 6, 22
trick or treating 14, 23
turnips 15

W
wallets 4, 5, 10–11
  see also magic wallet
waterproof materials 5, 11, 23
wood 7

Make and Use

Bags

& Purses

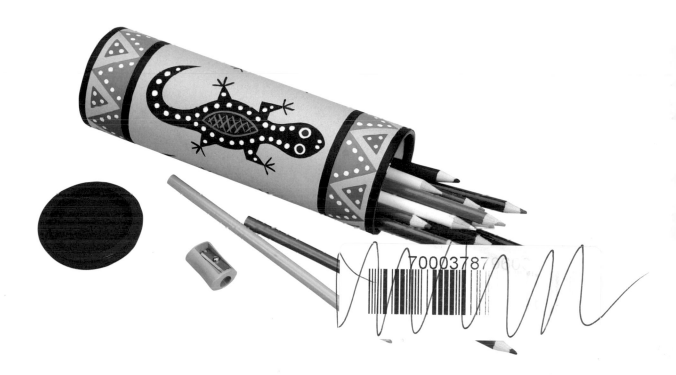

Anna-Marie D'Cruz

WAYLAND

First published in 2007
by Wayland

This paperback edition published
by Wayland in 2010

© Copyright 2007 Wayland

Wayland
338 Euston Road
London NW1 3BH

Wayland Australia
Level 17/207 Kent Street
Sydney NSW 2000

Senior Editor: Jennifer Schofield
Designer: Jason Billin
Project maker: Anna-Marie D'Cruz
Photographer: Chris Fairclough
Proofreader: Susie Brooks

Acknowledgements:
The Publisher would like to thank the following models:
Emel Augustin, Ammar Duffus, Teya Hutchison and Robin Stevens.

Picture Credits:
All photography Chris Fairclough except:
page 4 right: Werner Foreman/CORBIS; page 4 left: Richard
Cummins/CORBIS; page 5: right: Rob Howard/CORBIS; page 7
bottom right: Catherine Carnow/CORBIS

CIP data
 D'Cruz, Anna-Marie
    Purses and bags. - (Make and use)
    1. Handbags - Design and construction - Juvenile literature
    I. Title
    646.4'8

ISBN: 978 0 7502 6180 7

Printed in China

Wayland is a division of Hachette Children's Books,
an Hachette UK Company.
www.hachette.co.uk

Note to parents and teachers:
The projects in this book are designed
to be made by children. However, we
do recommend adult supervision at all
times as the Publisher cannot be held
responsible for any injury caused while
making the projects.